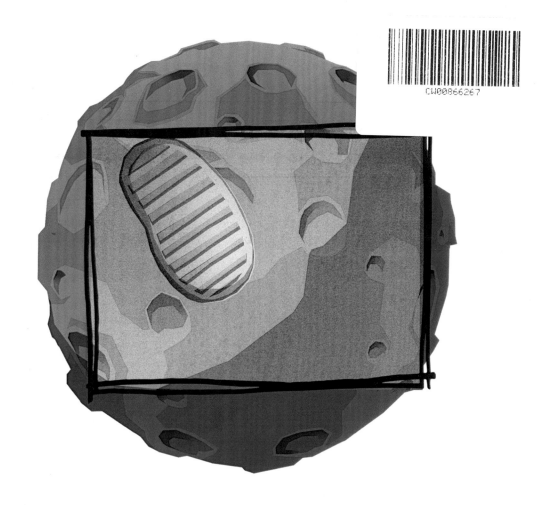

Apollo 11,
a Man on the Moon.

Humankind has traveled to all the
corners of the Earth,
but the most important voyage
was one that took us off
of the planet.

© Blue Planet Productions S.L
28017 Madrid

© Apollo 11, a Man on the Moon.
ISBN: 978-84-608-4930-8

Ilustrations: Melvira.
Cover and layout: Jesús Castillo.

For more information:
www.blueplanettales.com
info@blueplanettales.com

The first man on the moon

From the beginning of time, humans have watched the moon, wondering about that white sphere rotating in the sky. While observing, people thought, could it ever be possible to reach the moon? Those questions eventually led to humans to set foot on the moon.

Making a trip to the moon was very difficult, especially considering the era when the idea was first being proposed. They would need an extremely powerful rocket in order to burst through the Earth's gravity, land on the moon, allow astronauts to exit and collect samples, and make it back to Earth. In short: Mission Impossible!

In those days only two countries were capable of such a feat, the United States and the Soviet Union. The Soviets had taken the lead in the Space Race when they sent Laika the dog into space, and later, the first man: Yuri Gagarin.

American President John F. Kennedy put down a trump card in 1962 when he announced that we would send a man to the moon before the end of the decade.

In order to achieve this, he channeled enormous funding to NASA, whose scientists, engineers, astronauts and doctors dedicated hard work, knowledge, and put all hands on deck in order meet President Kennedy's goal.

Preparations lasted seven years. During this time, scientists calculated the power the rocket would need, the distance it would travel, the exact location for the moon landing, and all of the manuevers that would be required of the spacecraft. They carried out numerous experiments and selected a group of astronauts for the mission.

Amstrong

The astronauts were subjected to rigorous trainings and medical tests in preparation for the lunar mission. July 16, 1969 was set as the launch date for one of the most important missions of all times.

Commander Neil Armstrong, Colonel Buzz Aldrin and Lieutenant Colonel Michael Collins boarded the spacecraft equipped with fuel tanks

and a computer with less power than our modern phones have. At last, the countdown started and the first trip to the moon had begun!

People all over the whole world stood breathless, watching the launch on TV, as fire blasted from the booster rockets. Apollo 11 slowly rose up from its launch site at Cape Canaveral, gathering strength and speed as it headed up into space towards the moon.

As the spacecraft soared away into the distant sky, Mission Control in Houston erupted in celebration. The lunar voyage had successfully completed one of its most dangerous stages: launching Apollo 11 with loaded fuel tanks. But a quiet tension soon set in at Mission Control because this was only the first of several challenges to be overcome; it was too early for victory celebrations.

Seconds after takeoff, empty tanks burned up at take-off were released and fell to the ocean. The second set of tanks were in use, thrusting the rocket away from the Earth at great speed. When the second tank was empty, the third stage was initiated, and the spacecraft reached tremendous velocities.

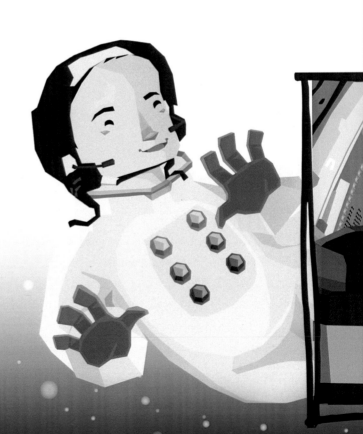

Suddenly, the astronauts felt like they were floating; in fact, they weren't strapped to their chairs. Apollo 11 had entered into Earth´s gravity-neutral orbit, rotating around the Earth and gathering the additional speed required to fire off towards the moon.

As the astronauts verified their location, a second set of orders came in from Mission Control. They were to begin another dangerous phase: Translunar injection.

Pointing at the moon, they quickly accelerated until reaching a speed of 28,000 mph, exiting Earth-orbit towards the moon.

Without fuel tanks, the lunar module slowly lost speed as the earth's gravity pulled at it, but then regained momentum as the moon's gravity began pulling them towards their destination.

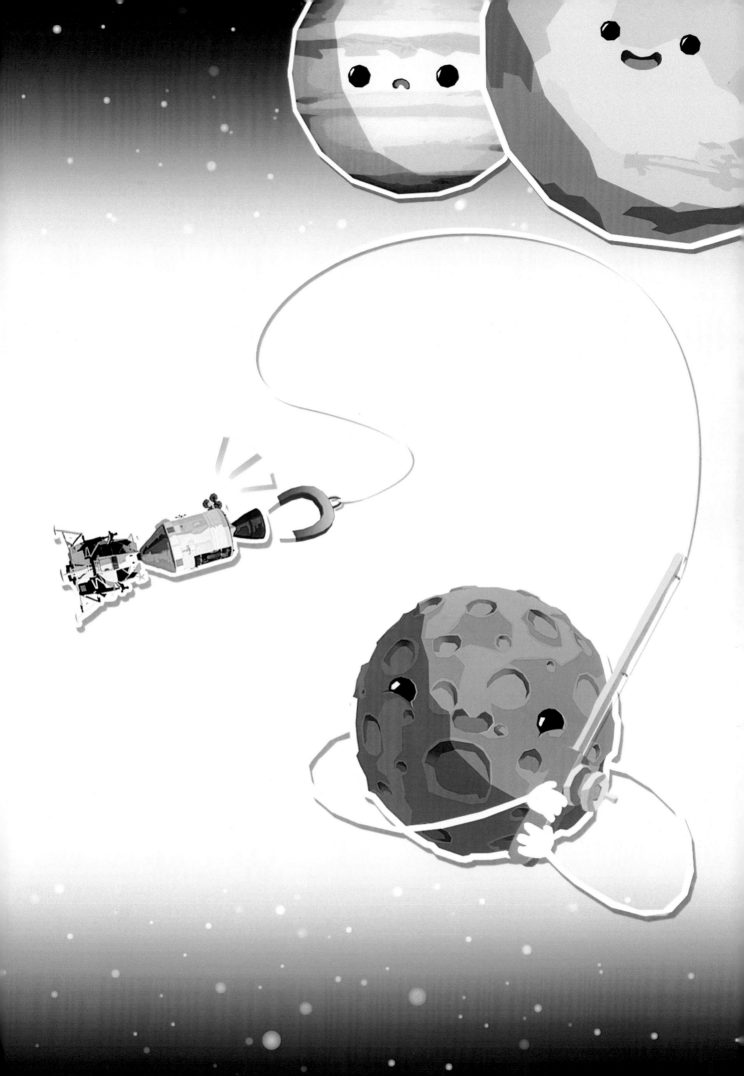

During the approach they orbited the moon 13 times, using its gravity to reduce speed. During this time, Armstrong and Aldrin switched over into the "Eagle", the lunar module to be used for the landing. Collins would remain orbiting in the spacecraft, awaiting their return. This was the most critical moment of the mission – the moon landing!

Armstrong and Aldrin slowly separated from the main spacecraft and began a rapid descent. They had to be very careful! The moon's surface was covered with rocks, and if they crashed into one, they would never return home. The module was heading straight for rocks when they had to quickly decide whether to abort the mission and go home or try to land in another part of the moon. It was a complex decision because not only was the mission in danger, but they feared for their lives.

Armstrong disconnected autopilot and took over the controls. He only had 30 seconds of fuel remaining in the tank. If it ran out, they would fall onto the moon.

They needed to find a safe place to touch down but they were rapidly descending and coming quite close to the ground. They had to slow down or else explode.

With only six feet to spare and very little fuel remaining in the tank, one of the module's three footpads touched down, soon followed by the rest.

Armstrong's voice sounded on the radio, "Houston, Tranquility Base here. The Eagle has landed."

Mission control in Houston again erupted with happiness. They had done it, they had achieved an unprecedented feat.
In order to exit the module, the men put on space suits to protect them from solar rays and lack of oxygen. Neil Armstrong would be first on the moon.

On July 21, 1969, Neil Armstrong changed the course of history. Opening up the door, he turned on the camera to share with the world what he saw in that moment. He then climbed down the ladder and with one foot on the moon he proclaimed, "That's one small step for man, one giant leap for mankind."

Aldrin came out behind him and they discovered the moon's low gravity, which permitted them to move freely despite their heavy suits. They had cameras and instruments to measure and collect photos and samples. After two and a half hours of exploring, they left behind a silicone disc with insignias and greetings in several languages, in honor of the first astronauts.

They also planted a U.S. flag
on the moon's surface just like mountain
climbers leave when they arrive
on a mountain peak for the first time.

With great emotion they boarded the Eagle so they could sleep before getting ready for the return trip home. After takeoff, their module flew back into the moon's orbit and approached the main rocket with great speed. Once directly in its path, they slowly approached until connecting with the main spacecraft.

After hugs and tears of joy, the three astronauts began their three-day journey home without any issues. The only problem arose when they approached Earth; a huge storm prevented them from landing as planned so they searched for another position to land near rescue boats – where the weather was calm.

They finally found a location near Hawaii. They shut off the brakes and gravity took them over the Pacific Ocean. One last complex phase of the mission lay before them: reentry into Earth's atmosphere.

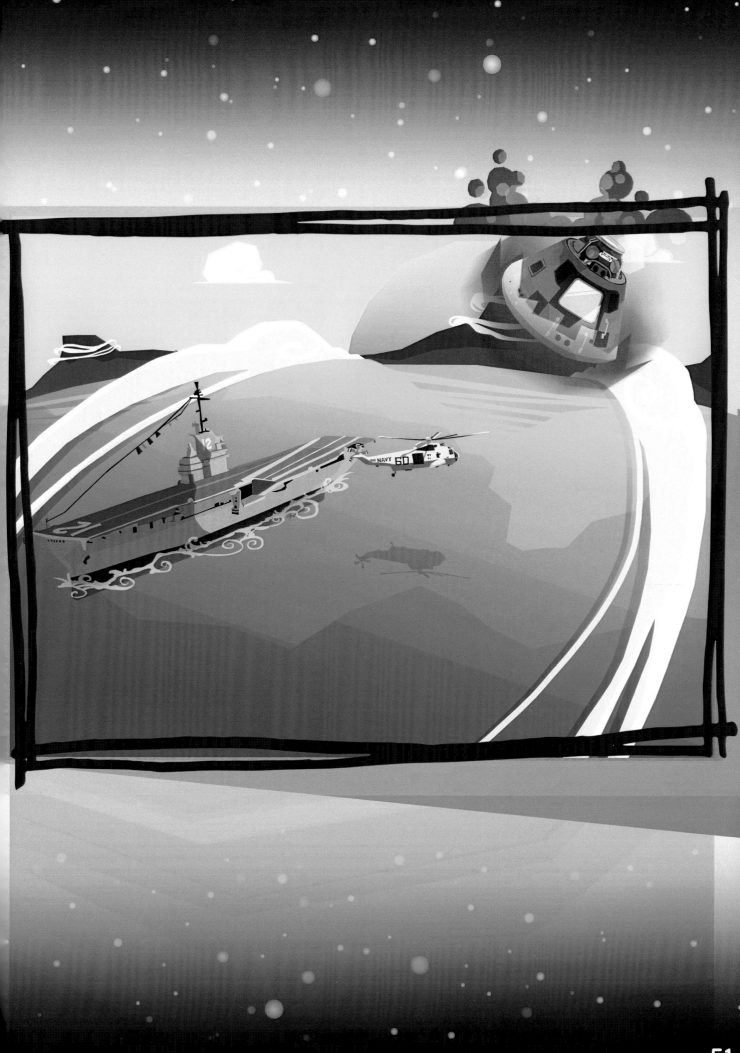

Friction caused temperatures to soar over 5,400 degrees and communication with Mission Control was lost.
For several minutes no one knew if they had successfully entered back into Earth's atmosphere or if they had disintegrated due to high temperatures. Suddenly, signals came in again from the rocket.
The astronauts had opened their parachutes and were slowly coming down.

After an eight day, three hour journey, the most important space mission of all times was finally home. The Apollo 11 expedition had begun with three astronauts and returned with three heroes: Armstrong, Collins and Aldrin. These men were more than heroes; they were the first men to reach the moon and come home to tell about it.

1. How was the moon formed?

A.　By a combination of planets
B.　By a combination of different types of rock
C.　After a planet crashed into Earth

2. What does a rocket need to do in order to gain enough speed to reach outer space?

A.　Power up its engines to maximum capacity
B.　Turn off its engines and use the pull of the moon's gravity
C.　Use the Earth's orbit

3. What are the hazards for humans on the moon?

A.　Solar rays and lack of oxygen
B.　Strange animals that might live there
C.　Extraterrestrials who have gotten there before us

4. Where is Cape Canaveral?

A.　In Russia
B.　In Houston
C.　In Florida

5. Who was the first human in space?

A.　Neil Armstrong
B.　Aldrin Collins
C.　Yuri Gagarin

6. Which American president proposed sending a man to the moon?

A.   Richard Nixon
B.   George Washington
C.   John F. Kennedy

7. What would have happened if the U.S. hadn't launched the Apollo mission?

A.   Humans wouldn't have arrived on the moon.
B.   The Russians would have gotten there first.
C.   All space missions would have been canceled.

8. What was the message that Neil Armstrong transmitted to Earth when he set foot on the moon?

A.   That's one small step for a man, one giant leap for mankind.
B.   We're here Martians!
C.   After this landing, the moon is all ours.

9. How many missions have landed on the moon, and with how many astronauts?

A.   1 mission and 2 astronauts
B.   3 missions and 6 astronauts
C.   6 missions and 12 astronauts

10. Where did astronauts work?

A.   At NASA
B.   At SANA
C.   In LAUSANA

1. How was the moon formed?

C.   After a planet crashed into Earth

2. What does a rocket need to do in order to gain enough speed to reach outer space?

C.   Use the Earth's orbit

3. What are the hazards for humans on the moon?

A.   Solar rays and lack of oxygen

4. Where is Cape Canaveral?

C.   In Florida

5. Who was the first human in space?

A.   Neil Armstrong

6. Which American president proposed sending a man to the moon?

C.   John F. Kennedy

7. What would have happened if the U.S. hadn't launched the Apollo mission?

B.   The Russians would have gotten there first

8. What was the message that Neil Armstrong transmitted to Earth when he set foot on the moon?

A.   That's one small step for a man, one giant leap for mankind

9. How many missions have landed on the moon, and with how many astronauts?

C.   6 missions and 12 astronauts

10. Where did astronauts work?

A.   At NASA